Ray

Thank you for being p[art of the]
CPulse Satisfaction Network.

Chrissy & the CPulse staff

The Customer Is Always Right!

The Customer Is Always Right!

Thought Provoking Insights on the Importance of Customer Satisfaction from Today's Business Leaders

Compiled by

Armen J. Kabodian

McGraw-Hill

New York San Francisco Washington, D.C. Auckland Bogotá
Caracas Lisbon London Madrid Mexico City Milan
Montreal New Delhi San Juan Singapore
Sydney Tokyo Toronto

McGraw-Hill

*A Division of The **McGraw·Hill** Companies*

3 4 5 6 7 8 9 0   DOC / DOC   9 0 0 9 8 7

ISBN 0-07-034209-1

The sponsoring editor for this book was Susan Barry, the editing supervisor was Fred Dahl, and the production supervisor was Donald F. Schmidt. It was set in Minion by Inkwell Publishing Services. The initial typesetting and editing was done by Karen Carlson, Document Design, Inc.

Printed and bound by R. R. Donnelley & Sons Co.

This book is dedicated to
my family,
my friends, and
my Customers.

— Armen

Contents

Introduction

The global marketplace continues to be very competitive. Businesses have been challenged to increase their levels of quality, improve their product designs, and decrease their product development cycle times. Significant progress has been made in these areas, but one of the most important objectives in the marketplace today is providing total customer satisfaction.

What is *customer satisfaction*?

There are many perspectives and opinions on the topic of customer satisfaction, but there is no official definition. Definitions vary, based on individual experiences and expectations. Therefore, the subjectivity of customer satisfaction has created a challenge for many individuals and businesses to overcome. Many have asked, "If we don't know the definition of customer satisfaction, how can it ever be achieved?"

To help define the meaning of customer satisfaction, I requested quotes and comments on the topic from leaders in business and industry, heads of government and public institutions, and consumer advocates. The number of requests that I sent exceeded 1000. My requests went to organizations of all sizes, to a variety of industries, and to many individuals of various cultures and countries. The responses to my requests have been compiled in *The Customer Is Always Right!*

The benefits that I received as a result of this project were that I:

✔ Gained a better appreciation for the personal aspect of customer satisfaction.

✔ Have an enhanced understanding of the commitment to customer satisfaction in the marketplace.

✔ Learned that providing customer satisfaction is just one characteristic of a customer-driven organization.

✔ Was reminded of the importance of *my Customers*.

I hope that, by providing you with this collection of comments and perspectives, you will also benefit. If this book can increase the level of overall service and customer satisfaction that you provide — and in the long-run receive as a consumer — my objective will have been met.

ARMEN J. KABODIAN

Acknowledgments

I am deeply grateful to the many leaders who provided their ideas and perspectives for this work. Thank you for your words of wisdom.

This work is the result of the support and cooperation of my wonderful wife Belinda. Thank you for your encouragement, patience, and love.

To Ariana and Margaux: Thank you for your smiles, laughs, hugs, and kisses. I think you're *great!*

The Customer Is Always Right!

Dear Armen,

The road to real customer satisfaction begins
with sincerity and integrity,
followed by hard work
and dedication for the long haul.

With love,
Dad

1

It's no longer a matter of customer satisfaction.
At 1-800-FLOWERS we strive for
"Customer Jubilation."
Every one of our employees is challenged to give
the customer something to brag about.
That creates word-of-mouth (WOM)
and it's good old WOM that makes us
more profitable, able to attract great talent, and
assures us a corporate culture
that is prideful and motivated.
It's a great cycle.

Jim F. McCann
President
1-800 Flowers, Inc.
Floral and gift retailer

Knowing your customer is the
first step in attaining customer satisfaction.
From there you can move toward
improving operational processes
that touch customers at various points
in the business relationship.
It's surprisingly challenging,
but essential,
to answer basic questions first.

Daniel P. Amos
President & C.E.O.
AFLAC, Inc.
Supplemental insurance and television stations

"Customer satisfaction"
is the customer's belief that
we are trustworthy
and that we exert real effort
to give value for what we charge.

Benjamin F. Edwards III
Chairman, President & C.E.O.
A. G. Edwards & Sons, Inc.
Securities investment

Today, satisfying
customers is not enough.
We must focus on
making our customers successful.
That means anticipating their needs
and surrounding them with
a full circle of service
making it easy for them to
justify, acquire, install, operate,
maintain and upgrade
our products over the lifetime
of those products.

Jodie K. Glore
President
Allen-Bradley Co.
Automation controls

5

Throughout the company,
we are no longer measuring
results against our expectations.
Because our opinions don't count.
They are irrelevant.
It's only the *customers'* expectations that matter.
Say we accomplish some task
93 percent of the time.
We don't take it upon ourselves to move our goal to
95 percent. Instead we ask customers what they need.
Maybe they think it's
essential for us to be at 100 percent.
Or maybe 30 percent would be more adequate.
They call the shots.

Richard C. Notebaert
Chairman & C.E.O.
Ameritech Corporation
Telecommunications/cellular/pagers/software

6

Manufacturers are responsible for
guaranteeing that
their customers are satisfied.
The goal is to exceed customer
expectations on what they value most.
At Amway, our money-back
Customer Satisfaction Guarantee
is our assurance that customers
receive full value
on the purchase of our products.

Dick DeVos
President
Amway Corporation
Direct selling

No matter how
technology and regulatory change
transform this market,
the winners will be people
who remember they're in business
to delight the customer.
You can never be good enough
at customer satisfaction.

Robert E. Allen
Chairman & C.E.O.
AT&T
Information products and services

In the end,
it is the *CUSTOMER'S* perception
that matters!
Delivering what *WE* think
is superior customer service
makes no difference at all.

Larry Dorfman
President & C.E.O.
Automobile Protection Corp. — APCO
Vehicle service contracts administrator

Make serving the customer
an obsession.

Dr. R. L. Qualls
President & C.E.O.
Baldor Electric Company
Electric motors and drives

10

Our mission states that
customer relationships are the source of all value.
A people-focused quality culture is
a critical business strategy,
just like sound financial performance.
Quality isn't easy,
but it's the right thing to do,
and a competitive advantage
for our business environment —
now and in the future.

Lawrence M. Johnson
Chairman & C.E.O.
Bancorp Hawaii, Inc.
Financial services

In the last analysis, it is
the customer and only the customer
who knows how
to improve customer service.
So in order to maintain and improve
a high level of satisfaction, we must
cautiously measure the quality
of service our customers receive,
as they perceive it.
Anything else is simply guesswork.

Matthew W. Barrett
Chairman & C.E.O.
Bank of Montreal
Financial service products

The polling place of the retail business
is at the cash registers.
Here, Customer Satisfaction
can be easily measured
in terms of both the size and
the frequency of the transactions.
There is no such thing as
customer "dissatisfaction"
in the competitive world of retailing.

Leonard Riggio
Chairman & C.E.O.
Barnes & Noble Inc.
Booksellers/bookstores

Customers don't care how big you are.
They don't care about
organizational charts or
how many divisions you have.
They want the person
standing in front of them
to be able to solve their problems.

Vernon R. Loucks Jr.
Chairman & C.E.O.
Baxter International Inc.
Health-care products and services

Customers are satisfied
when they get what they expect,
both with regard to results and behavior.
Creating satisfied customers
requires that expectations
about performance and
about the nature of the relationship
be *managed* and *met*.
We have satisfied customers
because we get the job done *and*
because we are responsive.

James E. Cayne
President & C.E.O.
Bear, Stearns & Co., Inc.
Investment banking

15

Given a level playing field on product quality,
you must provide
complete customer satisfaction
to insure repeat purchases.
Customer satisfaction is the
sum total of the buying experience.
In other words,
the buyer must feel satisfied every step of the way:
from the time of purchase through
the full life of the product.
Taking care of customer satisfaction
is job security for all of us.

Raymond F. Winter
President & C.O.O.
BIC Corporation
Consumer products: writing instruments; lighters; shavers; correction fluids

"Customer Satisfaction"
is the true fuel
of the free enterprise system.
In a free market environment,
traditional indicators of success,
such as sales and market share growth,
are only indicators of a company's level of
"Customer Satisfaction."

Dane A. Miller
President & C.E.O.
Biomet, Inc.
Orthopedic implants and supplies

17

The true measure of
a company's value to society
— and to its ownership —
is customer satisfaction.
Without it, no business can survive,
provide jobs, or enrich the lives
of those it seeks to serve.
Sincerely practiced,
it can energize the most positive
advertising vehicle at our disposal —
word of mouth.

H. Wayne Huizenga
Chairman & C.E.O.
Blockbuster Entertainment Corporation
*Home video and prerecorded music retailer, filmed entertainment production and distribution,
interactive entertainment software, children's indoor playgrounds*

A marketer can experience
"customer satisfaction" only when
the product or service meets or exceeds
customer expectations.
In this respect, the definitions of
"quality" and "customer service"
are similar.
The correct measure for this business parameter
should be "customer retention"
which quantifies the percent of customers
returning to purchase a
product or service.

Sunil Kumar
President
Bridgestone/Firestone, Tire Sales Co.
Tires and auto service

19

The universe of individuals
who can objectively evaluate
the quality of your services
is minuscule.
However, everyone can
make a judgment
based on how they were treated,
what they felt about it —
how prompt, efficient,
professional, courteous,
and so forth you were.

Peter A. Michel
President & C.E.O.
Brink's Home Security, Inc.
Residential security services

20

Effective communication is the key
to providing quality. Typically, not
enough effort is made among team members
to communicate prior to starting a project.
As a result, errors occur and adversarial
relationships develop. The owner's needs get lost ...
This is why, before a project starts, we gather every
team member to mutually develop a delivery process
that is responsive to the owner's expectations. At the
end of this effort, everyone understands his or her role
and how each individual's work affects other project
team members. Hence, the focus is shifted from
working individually to how we as a team can provide
greater value to the owner.
Everyone comes out a winner.

George E. Day, Jr., AIA
President & C.E.O.
BSW International
Architecture/engineering firm

Customer satisfaction is
generated by the ability to
make your customer feel *special,*
as if each is your *only* customer
and you are totally dedicated
to serving their every wish and keeping
them happy at *all* times.
Listen to what your customer wants
and then satisfy their needs.

James B. Miller
Chairman & C.E.O.
B.T. Miller Business Systems, Inc.
Office supplies/office furniture

At Burger King,
we have learned that
consumers' demands are very basic.
They want high quality food,
served in a fast, friendly atmosphere,
at a good value.
Our goal is to exceed customers' expectations
in each of these areas
by focusing on a "back to basics" approach
at each and every
Burger King restaurant
around the world.

Robert C. Lowes
Chief Executive Officer
Burger King Corporation
Quick service restaurants

Customer Satisfaction is the oxygen of life
at *Worth Magazine.*
In everything we do,
customer satisfaction is Job One.
From the beginning, I put my phone number
in my "Forward Thinking" column;
I read and respond to every letter
that *Worth Magazine* receives;
and I am constantly watching our renewal rates.
Why? Because a satisfied reader
is not only money in the bank,
but the emotional currency that
makes publishing *Worth Magazine*
truly worthwhile.

W. Randall Jones
Founder & C.E.O.
Capital Publishing Company, Inc.
Worth Magazine

Moving products
is simply not enough in today's
rapidly changing transportation industry.
Meeting client requirements from
an information technology and customer service
perspective is critical in order for
rapid replenishment, quick response, and
just-in-time inventory programs to be successful.
Such programs, along with continuing
deregulation, have required a total reengineering
of the less-than-truckload transportation industry.
This metamorphosis will continue through the year
2000, fueled by both domestic and international
customer requirements.

Lary R. Scott
Chairman & C.E.O.
Carolina Freight Corporation
Transportation (truck)

It is important that we
understand customer satisfaction
from the customer's viewpoint.
Their view should be surveyed periodically,
care should be taken
to understand what they say, and
we should respond accordingly.

George W. Off
President & C.E.O.
Catalina Marketing Corporation
Electronic marketing services

26

A company that believes
"customer satisfaction"
is their primary goal
is on their way out of business.
It's not enough in today's
quality service culture to meet
the customer's expectations;
to be an industry leader,
it is imperative that you
exceed their expectations and
leave them with a wow!

Richard J. Loughlin
President & C.E.O.
Century 21 Real Estate Corp.
Real estate franchising

Be fair, empathetic and responsive
in serving our customers.
Respect and reinforce your fellow employees
and the power of teamwork.
Strive relentlessly to improve
what we do and how we do it.
Always earn and be worthy of
our customer's trust.

from The Vision and Values of our Company by:
Charles R. Schwab
Chairman & C.E.O.
Charles Schwab & Co. Inc.
Financial services

Customers are becoming increasingly
discriminating in the marketplace.
Our job is to understand
what brings value to our customers
and then provide this
better than our competition.
Customer satisfaction is the
result of this transaction.

Kenneth T. Derr
Chairman & C.E.O.
Chevron Corporation
Petroleum-based products and services

Customer satisfaction
is the ultimate measure
of everything we do,
from the initial design of a car or truck
to the little pang of regret the owner feels
when they trade them in.

Robert J. Eaton
Chairman & C.E.O.
Chrysler Corporation
Passenger cars and light trucks

We're not just in the car business,
we're in the business
of providing customer satisfaction
in personal transportation.

Robert J. Eaton
Chairman & C.E.O.
Chrysler Corporation
Passenger cars and light trucks

31

Customers, internal or external, feel good
when they are presented
with quality from their supplier.
The producer of quality feels good
as a result of his accomplishment
and enjoys a satisfying relationship
with his customer.

The culture evolving in this environment
feeds on itself in a very positive manner
causing suppliers, producers, and customers
to enjoy a sense of fulfillment, self worth
and self esteem, or what we typically call
"customer satisfaction."

James L. Clayton
Chairman & C.E.O.
Clayton Homes, Inc.
Manufactured homes

Customer satisfaction is
"meeting customer needs
in a timely and cost effective way."

Charles M. Leighton
Founder & C.E.O.
CML Group, Inc.
Consumer products: NordicTrack, Nature Company,
Smith & Hawken, Britches of Georgetown

Today, having great
products isn't enough.
Customers are looking for that
"feel good" experience!
Because coffee is a
warm, friendly beverage,
we should also treat our customers
as special visitors to our home.
Then they will want to come back
again and again.

JoAnne Shaw
President
The Coffee Beanery, Ltd.
Specialty coffee and related products

We are committed to ensuring
that consumers can continue to trust
Colgate products for their reliability, quality and
superior performance.
Since our business is consumer products,
our success depends upon consumer satisfaction,
trust and goodwill . . .
We also believe that consumer opinions, concerns
and inquiries communicated to the Company
regarding our products are important
sources of information.
Consumer needs are constantly changing, so we must
continually listen to what people want and use our
creativity to satisfy these changing needs.

from the Colgate-Palmolive Company
Code of Conduct
Colgate-Palmolive Company
Consumer products

In years past, an electric utility's
customers did business with it
because they had to.
There was no other choice.
In the deregulated energy marketplace
of the future, customers will deal
with us because they want to,
because we have met
and continue to meet their needs
better than anyone else.

James J. O'Connor
Chairman & C.E.O.
Commonwealth Edison Company
Electric utility

"Customer Satisfaction" is:
The first step in transforming
a product user into
a *loyal* customer.

Eckhard Pfeiffer
President & C.E.O.
Compaq Computer Corporation
World's largest supplier of personal computers

Our customers are
the American people.
We have promised them that
we will reinvent government
so that it works better and costs less.
That means the Consumer Product Safety
Commission must satisfy the public
that every action we take
and every dollar we spend
prevents unnecessary injuries and deaths.

Ann Brown
Chairman
Consumer Product Safety Commission
Protecting the American public from hazardous consumer products

Customers are satisfied
when they are courteously treated;
when the products and services they buy are
of good quality, safe, and effective for
the purposes to be served;
when the costs are fair and reasonably reflect
the value received;
when the advertisements are honest and informative;
and when any complaints they may have are
respectfully received, and appropriately redressed.
Taken together, customers are satisfied
when they operate in a marketplace
they find to be fair, ethical, and
responsive to their needs.

Rhoda H. Karpatkin
President
Consumers Union
Publisher of Consumer Reports *magazine*

The atmosphere and service
in the stores is what determines
the customer satisfaction level.
It's really the total atmosphere that
we give to people in the stores —
that we are there to help them and to serve them
and make sure their purchase is
a good purchase for them.
Once that is executed and executed well,
nobody can take that away from you.
It's your total personality in the
retail business that counts
and that total execution
that makes your business unique.

Gordon I. Segal
Chief Executive Officer
Crate & Barrel
Housewares and home furnishings retailer

Regardless of the size of a service company,
a high degree of Customer Satisfaction
will be maintained as long as
employees at all levels remain mindful
of the maxim that
"the customer is always right."
If you determine that
a customer is not right, then,
for all intents and purposes,
you have already terminated
your relationship with that customer.

John Olsen
Chairman & C.E.O.
Cunard Line Limited
Cruise line

I believe you have attained
"customer satisfaction"
when customers return to your store
because they *want* to
not because they have to.

Richard T. Takata
President & C.O.O.
Eagle Hardware & Garden, Inc.
Home improvement retailer

The spin-off from
Eastman Kodak Company
and winning the
Malcolm Baldrige National Quality Award
made 1993 a big year
for Eastman Chemical Company.
People often ask what we are going to do
for an encore.
Our answer is summed up in two words:
CUSTOMER SATISFACTION.

Earnest Deavenport
Chairman & C.E.O.
Eastman Chemical Company
International manufacturer of plastics, chemicals, and fibers

"Customer Satisfaction" is:
the superordinate objective of
any well run business.
It must be the focus of a
never ending pursuit that includes
excellence in quality, cycle time and
product and service leadership.
The result of this relentless focus will be
greater growth, greater marketshare
and improved profitability.

George M. C. Fisher
President, Chairman & C.E.O.
Eastman Kodak Co., Inc.
World's leader in imaging

44

We can no longer be content with
giving our customers what they want.
Our mandate for quality
in the 1990s requires that we
exceed our customers' expectations.
We must provide a level of quality
that provides no less than
customer delight.

William E. Butler
Chairman & C.E.O.
Eaton Corporation
*Manufacturer of vehicle components and electrical
and electronic controls*

When he opened his first store
in 1920, Eddie Bauer,
the founder of our company,
wrote Our Creed.
Today, nearly three-quarters of a century later,
this single statement still exemplifies
the meaning of Customer Satisfaction
and is our final measurement of success:
"To give you such outstanding quality,
value, service and guarantee
that we may be worthy of
your high esteem."

Richard Fersch
President
Eddie Bauer, Inc.
Specialty retail

46

At EDS, performance
is the key to attracting and retaining customers.
CUSTOMER SATISFACTION
is the heart of this process.

EDS people and processes combine
to understand and deliver to the needs,
requirements and expectations
of our customers.

Our goal is to generate true
CUSTOMER SATISFACTION
and thereby earn customer loyalty.

Lester M. Alberthal, Jr.
Chairman, President & C.E.O.
Electronic Data Systems Corporation
Global information services

As global competition increases,
successful companies will need
to maintain a unique edge.
That edge is uncompromised,
total customer satisfaction.
Exemplified by international quality programs,
U.S. businesses are being judged
by their ability to provide
comprehensive customer solutions.
Failure to provide such services
will result in failure to do business.

David S. Deutsch
President
Executrain
Computer training

"Customer Satisfaction" is:
Doing all things desired by customers
so as to insure their repurchase
of the product or service
at every future opportunity.
At FedEx 100% customer satisfaction
is an integral part of our
corporate mission statement!

Frederick W. Smith
President, Chairman & C.E.O.
Federal Express Corporation
Express transport and logistics

49

The challenge to our bank is
to link quality service efforts
to bottom line results.
Measuring whether increased revenues
and customer retention
result from outstanding quality service
or factors such as competitive pricing is vital.
We need a Return on Equity measure
as much as a
Return on Investment measure.

Nancy L. Singer
President & C.E.O.
First of America Bank — Northeast Illinois, N.A.
Commercial banking, including retail services

50

At Fluor Corporation, we've always strived
to deliver "customer satisfaction,"
yet in our rapidly changing and intensely competitive
global marketplace,
it's become increasingly more challenging.
Today, we stay closer to our customers than ever
before, listening to them, and finding innovative ways
to solve their problems and create value.
We've also learned a great deal from customer
satisfaction surveys.
They've prompted us to reengineer our organization
so we can become
"better, faster, cheaper, and safer"
in the way we deliver our services to clients.

Leslie G. McCraw
Chairman & C.E.O.
Fluor Corporation
Engineering, construction and diversified services

A journalist told me recently,
"You talk so much about
customer satisfaction that
you'd think Ford created it."
I told him, "It's just the opposite:
Ford didn't create customer satisfaction —
customer satisfaction created Ford."
And I'm sure every successful
global company can say the same.
Companies that satisfy customers best,
whether they're high-tech or
hand crafts, have the
global advantage.

Louis R. Ross
Vice Chairman & Chief Technical Officer
The Ford Motor Company
Automobile manufacturer and financial services

Our customers worldwide
expect better and better quality
every model year.
And it's the nature of
competition in business today that
if you're not getting better
you're getting behind.

Alexander J. Trotman
Chairman, President & C.E.O.
The Ford Motor Company
Automobile manufacturer and financial services

Customer Satisfaction:
Starts with defining the customer
and his expectations of the product.
Problems evolve when a business
incorrectly designs the product
based upon the businessman's design
without clearly researching the customer's desires.
If the product is improperly sold,
customers can have different expectations
of the product from its design.

Peter N. Brown
President
Four Seasons Group, Inc.
Resort development

Companies spend too much time
trying to satisfy their customers.
Time would be better spent
satisfying themselves.
Customer satisfaction
becomes irrelevant when
your customers' concerns
become your own concerns.
Companies can then act in their own
guiltless self-interests each day,
and their customers will be well served.

Tim Hudson
President
Fourth Wave Technologies/USConnect
Computer services

A customer is really satisfied
when he or she not only comes back
but brings someone with them.

Hyrum W. Smith
Chairman & C.E.O.
Franklin Quest Company
Time management products and services

Our Mission Statement says it all:
"To best satisfy America's snacking needs
by providing fun foods
within arms' reach."

Steve Reinemund
Chairman & C.E.O.
Frito-Lay, Inc.
America's largest snack food company

I try to treat every customer
like I used to treat my grandmother.
When she was alive, and I was with her,
I just shut up, listened to her, and kept trying
to give her what she asked for until I was successful.
Because I loved her and had never won an
argument with her, I didn't waste time
worrying about *why* she wanted me to
dig the family silver out from its basement hiding
place to eat her oatmeal with, or why I must always
put the dish soap in *before* I started filling the
kitchen sink with hot water.
I just did it her way, because she wanted me to.

Rick Stewart
Chief Executive Officer
Frontier Cooperative Herbs
Herbs, spices, essential oils, and roasted coffee

I get a thousand opportunities a year
to make a decision in favor of
the customer.
Each time I blow it, it costs me
about $10,000 in lost sales.
At that price — *of course*
the customer is always right.

Rick Stewart
Chief Executive Officer
Frontier Cooperative Herbs
Herbs, spices, essential oils, and roasted coffee

Did you ever try to outsmart your
17 year old daughter?
Well, don't try to outsmart
your customers, either.

Rick Stewart
Chief Executive Officer
Frontier Cooperative Herbs
Herbs, spices, essential oils, and roasted coffee

In today's world, the will to win
is more than just wanting to win.
It's a matter of focusing all assets and all decisions
on the customer.
The customer is the ultimate arbiter
of success or failure.
Winning in the marketplace is
a matter of providing
superior customer value and service.

John F. Smith, Jr.
C.E.O. & President
General Motors Corporation
Automotive vehicles

We know that
every customer
has many other places to take
his or her business if we fall short.
All of the soul-searching
and all of the change
that GM has been going through
is driven by the realization that
the company that wins is the one
that is most in touch with
the customer.

John F. Smith, Jr.
C.E.O. & President
General Motors Corporation
Automotive vehicles

Customer service means
having competent and knowledgeable staffers
who provide customers with
friendly, helpful service.
It means offering
quality products and services
that exceed customer expectations.
And, it means having a mechanism in place
to be responsive to customer
inquiries and concerns.

Israel Cohen
Chairman & C.E.O.
Giant Food, Inc.
Grocery retailer

I am convinced that organizations
with their sights set on achieving
customer satisfaction are doomed
since they are merely aiming
to meet customer expectations.
To prosper in the 90's you must aim higher.
You must exceed
customers' expectations — consistently.
At GMC Truck we call this striving for
Customer Enthusiasm ... Always!

Roy S. Roberts
Vice President & General Manager
GMC Truck Division, General Motors Corporation
GMC truck products

As businesses improve their competitive position
through restructuring, cost reduction,
improved quality, productivity improvements
and capital investment,
the battle for overall success must move
from the foundry and factory floors
to the sales and marketing arena.
Success hinges on development of
new products/services and new markets
that satisfy customer needs.

Stanley C. Gault
Chairman & C.E.O.
Goodyear Tire & Rubber Company
Tires, oil transportation, rubber, and chemical products

"Customer Satisfaction" is
that elusive goal of the retailer
to provide products and services
which keep patrons coming back.
It's not achieved through any one thing.
Rather, it's a combination of
service, products, accessibility,
knowledgeable sales personnel, and the impression
when a customer walks through the door
which prompts him or her to say to friends,
"Hey, have you been to Play It Again Sports®?
Let me tell you about the
great experience I had there."

Ronald G. Olson
President & C.E.O.
Grow Biz International, Inc.
Franchise retail stores

Customer Satisfaction is
not a listing of criteria to be met,
but rather an attitude —
Best summed in the phrase
"Exceed Expectations".

William H. Williams
President
Harry & David
Mail order

67

Our job is all about
putting smiles on the faces of children
who play with our toys and games.
In order to do that,
you'd better be serious
about customer satisfaction, and
— believe me —
at Hasbro we are.

Alan G. Hassenfeld
Chairman & C.E.O.
Hasbro, Inc.
*Leading manufacturer and marketer of toys, games,
puzzles, and infant care products*

We are convinced
that the success of our business depends
on satisfied customers.
We achieve their satisfaction
by quickly translating their needs
into products and services that are world class
and that emphasize quality, design,
innovation, and value.

Richard G. Haworth
Chairman & C.E.O.
Haworth, Inc.
Office systems furniture

Today, satisfying customers
goes beyond meeting their needs
and exceeding their expectations.
Satisfying a customer should
involve helping them to grow
by anticipating their needs.

Michael A. Volkema
President & C.E.O.
Herman Miller, Inc.
Office furniture and office furniture management

Customer satisfaction is
THE most critical success factor
in any business enterprise.
Without it, one cannot achieve
the benefits of customer loyalty —
repeat business, referrals
and reduced marketing costs.

Frank A. Olson
Chairman & C.E.O.
The Hertz Corporation
Car rental

Yes, it is true we're in the
business and recreational hospitality business,
but we never forget
that above all, we're in the
customer satisfaction business.
In our industry, customer service
is the key determinant
for a company's ultimate success.

Barron Hilton
Chairman of the Board
Hilton Hotels Corporation
Hospitality

A smile costs nothing —
and in the hospitality industry,
it means everything.

Bryan D. Langton
Chairman & C.E.O.
Holiday Inn Worldwide
Hotels

We help people from all walks of life
attain the dream of home ownership
by providing quality home improvement products
at affordable prices.
But, just as important, we back it up
with exceptional service, second-to-none.
Working in a positive environment
fosters good will.
Being friendly and helpful is contagious —
it creates bonds of trust with customers.
If we can solve a home improvement problem
for a customer, it makes our day.

Bernard Marcus
Chairman & C.E.O.
The Home Depot
Home improvement retail

What Hughes Electronics must be
more than anything else is
"a customer company."
Our customers will direct our technology.
Our customers will determine our diversification.
Our customers will dictate our growth.

C. Michael Armstrong
Chairman & C.E.O.
Hughes Electronics Corporation
Automotive, defense, telecommunications, and space electronics

Everything starts with the Customer.

Louis V. Gerstner, Jr.
Chairman & C.E.O.
IBM Corporation
Advanced information technology solutions

Our primary measures of success
are customer satisfaction and
shareholder value.

Louis V. Gerstner, Jr.
Chairman & C.E.O.
IBM Corporation
Advanced information technology solutions

We've got to get back to
a fundamental issue, and that is:
We all work first for the customer.

Louis V. Gerstner, Jr.
Chairman & C.E.O.
IBM Corporation
Advanced information technology solutions

In the 90s,
companies that understand and embrace
individualized customer needs
will clearly dominate.
From this trend,
a new economy is emerging
in which the integration of
technology and business process is
revolutionizing previous notions of
production and supply.

Rick Inatome
Chairman
Inacom Corporation
*Marketers of computers and communications
systems and services*

Customer satisfaction is achieved
when the customer becomes convinced
through your performance that
the value he enjoys from your goods and services
exceeds all other options
and that his business with you
is important to you and is appreciated.

Henry M. Rowan
President
Inductotherm Industries, Inc.
Family of companies

"Customer Satisfaction" is:
Teaching every member of our organization,
from the C.E.O. to the maintenance person,
the philosophy of good customer service
and practicing this philosophy.
In simple terms, the concept is to ensure that
customers are satisfied and
to strive to go beyond their expectations.

David Lubetkin
President
Industrial Edge USA
*Supply maintenance products to the multi housing
industry (apartment houses)*

Our ultimate success depends
on understanding the complexities
of what makes people satisfied or dissatisfied,
and then acting on that knowledge.

Dr. David M. Lawrence
Chairman & C.E.O.
Kaiser Permanente
Health care

82

Customer satisfaction
means recognizing and valuing
lifelong partnerships with every customer;
creating and enhancing
bonds of respect and consideration
with every customer contact;
attending to the smallest detail of the shortest
phone call, and the entire conversation of the
longest customer meeting.
In summary, *customer satisfaction is exceeding
customer expectations.*

Richard L. Chitty
Vice President, Service, Parts & Customer Satisfaction
Lexus
Luxury automobiles

83

Customer satisfaction
has only two requirements.
Delivery of what is promised
when it is promised is one.
Answering customers' questions
accurately when they ask them
is the other.

Gary L. Countryman
Chairman & C.E.O.
Liberty Mutual Insurance Company
Insurance

The customer is always right!

Lillian Vernon
Chairperson & C.E.O.
Lillian Vernon Corporation
Gifts/mail order

Quality is the essential element
in gaining a customer's trust.
To forfeit it once
is to lose it forever.

Lillian Vernon
Chairperson & C.E.O.
Lillian Vernon Corporation
Gifts/mail order

I never sell my customers short
or underestimate their desire
for good quality, taste and style.

Lillian Vernon
Chairperson & C.E.O.
Lillian Vernon Corporation
Gifts/mail order

Our firm can help a company
build awareness, posture and position,
reeducate and redefine.
But unless we know
what the customer wants
and how to deliver it,
the rest of this stuff doesn't
mean a whole lot.
Too many companies still believe that
the right logo and ad campaign
are all it takes.
But they don't know how to make
a customer want to come back.

Linda A. Wasche
President
LW Marketworks, Inc.
Marketing communications/ public relations consultancy

At MBE, we measure Customer Satisfaction
by the degree to which our service
exceeds customer expectations.
Initially exceeding expectations was easy
since customers were accustomed
to dealing with the US Post Office.
Over the past few years however,
our Customers have come to expect better service.
Our goal is to maintain a high level
of Customer Satisfaction
by continually delivering "shockingly good service."

Anthony Desio
President & C.E.O.
Mail Boxes Etc., Inc.
*World's largest franchisor of postal, business, and communications
retail service centers*

At Mary Kay,
our customer is
our sales force, and it is our
Beauty Consultants and Directors
who make our jobs possible.
We must always remember that
business will continue
to go where invited and
return where appreciated —
and that reputations will continue to
be made by many acts,
but lost by only one.

Mary Kay Ash
Chairman Emeritus
Mary Kay Cosmetics, Inc.
Direct selling skin care and color cosmetics

We must remember that
people will continue business
with those who give good service,
and certainly there is never a
traffic jam on that extra mile.
Performance will continue to outsell promises.
Enthusiasm will be as contagious as ever.
Know-how will surpass guess-how.
And trust, not tricks, will keep our customers loyal.

Mary Kay Ash
Chairman Emeritus
Mary Kay Cosmetics, Inc.
Direct selling skin care and color cosmetics

If you really want to know
what "customer satisfaction"
means in the payments business —
you'll have to ask our customers.
With payment technologies advancing
at such a rapid pace, you must
involve customers in all aspects of
product design and delivery
to ensure that their needs are met.

Arthur B. Ziegler
Chairman Emeritus
MasterCard International, Inc.
Payment services company

Turn on the customer,
make him or her feel special.
Treat all customers like you're
darn happy to have them in the store.
Never be satisfied.
And you do whatever you need to,
right at that point in time,
to make sure when that customer leaves
that McDonald's restaurant,
he or she is happy.

Michael R. Quinlan
Chairman & C.E.O.
McDonald's Corporation
Leading food service retailer in the global consumer marketplace

For a time, customer satisfaction
was synonymous with quality.
Not to downplay the need for quality,
but MCI has found that
customers don't buy on the basis of just quality.
Or just price, or just reputation,
or even on customer service.
Customers buy on the combination
of all those attributes —
what they perceive as value.
To win customers in the 90's,
you have to provide value that's
superior to the competition.

Bert C. Roberts, Jr.
Chairman & C.E.O.
MCI Communications Corporation
International voice and data telecommunications services

MCI believes that
market share will be won by companies
that deliver what customers want . . .
and not necessarily by those who
put together the biggest deal.

Bert C. Roberts, Jr.
Chairman & C.E.O.
MCI Communications Corporation
International voice and data telecommunications services

Many players come to the market
with a "monopoly mindset."
They think they know
what's best for customers,
even without asking them.
MCI knows that
what customers want is important.
We know how to find out
what they want, and we have
the resources to deliver it.

Bert C. Roberts, Jr.
Chairman & C.E.O.
MCI Communications Corporation
International voice and data telecommunications services

At Meineke, we aim
far higher than zero complaints.
Total customer satisfaction
isn't achieved when a
quiet customer never returns.
We want customers to be enthusiastically loyal,
to brag about Meineke,
and to know we value their input.
It's a question of learning
your customers' expectations . . .
and consistently surpassing them.

Ronald S. Smythe
President & C.E.O.
Meineke Discount Muffler Shops, Inc.
Nationwide chain of franchised muffler and brake shops

Customer satisfaction is
an essential, but invisible feature
of any successful product.

Takashi "Tachi" Kiuchi
Chairman & C.E.O.
Mitsubishi Electric America
Electronics

"WOW" the customer —
whatever it takes.
Redo the order, make a settlement,
personally deliver the photos.
We want our customer to say
"WOW, I can't believe
what Moto does to make me happy."

Michael Adler
President & C.E.O.
Moto Photo, Inc.
One-hour photo finishing and portrait studios

Customer Service
does not come from a manual . . . .
It comes from the heart.
When it comes to
taking care of the customer . . .
you can never do too much
and there is *NO* wrong way
if it comes from the heart!

Debra J. Fields
President
Mrs. Fields, Inc.
Market leader of fresh-baked cookies

We exist to serve our customers.
In pursuit of this
customer satisfaction vision directive
we will understand our customers' needs and
expectations as never before.
Based on this knowledge,
we will empower our people
to respond proactively
to serve customers.

D. Richard McFerson
President & C.E.O.
Nationwide Insurance
Insurance and financial services

All the resources
of a business organization
must focus on the customer.
Even the most indirect resource
must have a vision of its role in
customer satisfaction.

John H. Dasburg
President & C.E.O.
Northwest Airlines, Inc.
Transportation

Customer satisfaction begins *before* the sale.
In our case, customer satisfaction begins with
recruiting, training and educating each member of
the Northwestern Mutual sales force, which
consistently ranks as the finest in life insurance.
Customer satisfaction is further enhanced *during* the
sale, which must always be based on the customer's
needs. Finally, customer satisfaction means providing
excellent service for a *lifetime.*
A typical Northwestern Mutual policy owner will
remain our customer for 40 years or more. That's
why we focus on delivering the same fair and
equitable treatment — and the same excellent service
— to old and new policyowners alike.

James D. Ericson
President & C.E.O.
Northwestern Mutual Life
Life insurance

"Customer Satisfaction" is:
A quick response that more than meets
the customer's needs.

Lloyd P. Johnson
Chairman
Norwest Corporation
Banking

At NYNEX, we have a saying that
"Nobody wins until the customer wins,
and the way the customer wins
is through teamwork."
We are working very hard
to build a winning culture and organization
that embraces this total commitment
to customer satisfaction.

William C. Ferguson
Chairman & C.E.O.
NYNEX Corporation
Communications

In my career, I've not met many customers
who got out of bed in the morning
with the thought that "today I'm going to take
advantage of a retailer."
Recognizing that customers almost always
only want what is fair,
a company can economically do
just about anything it takes
to win customers over and retain them.
In the scheme of things, customer service is
one of a company's most cost-effective investments
in its future.

Michael Feuer
President & C.E.O.
OfficeMax, Inc.
Office product superstores

Satisfied Customers
are what keep us in business.

Barbara Hennigar
President
Oppenheimer Shareholder Services
A mutual fund service provider

Satisfied customers receive
high quality, an affordable price,
and life cycle service.
Oracle gauges our success as a company
by measuring how well we enable our customers
to confidently meet the tough challenges of
information technology.
Oracle is focused on improving every aspect
of our business so we can give
our customers absolutely the best
and most reliable mission-critical solutions.
Our customer's success is our success.

James A. Abrahamson
Former Chairman of the Board
Oracle Corporation
Computer software

In our company,
Customer Satisfaction is a philosophy.
We are guided by all we do,
dependent on customer satisfaction
being enhanced.
If a company in today's market
does not truly embrace this philosophy,
they will die.

David E. O'Reilly
President & C.E.O.
O'Reilly Automotive, Inc.
Specialty retailer of auto parts

At Owens-Corning,
we think Customer Satisfaction
is more accurately defined as
customer delight.
It is gained through providing
the highest quality, lowest cost products
combined with service beyond comparison.
The business cycle begins
when the customer places an order.
Customers do us a favor
when they place an order with us,
and we must delight them in order
to earn their repeat business.

Glen H. Hiner
Chairman & C.E.O.
Owens-Corning Fiberglas Corporation
World leader in advanced glass and composite materials

Customer satisfaction is
the complete harmony between
expectations and reality.

Alan Hoops
President & C.E.O.
PacifiCare Health Systems, Inc.
Health care services company

The hiring and training of people
that have the capacity and skill set
to deliver quality service
is the first step to customer satisfaction.

B. Thomas Golisano
Chairman, President & C.E.O.
Paychex, Inc.
Payroll service

I have a saying
attached to my wall which holds:
The value of pleasing a customer
is more important than the cost.
I think that says it all.
Good customer satisfaction,
whether it is in the manufacturing,
retailing or service industry,
is the bedrock of any business
if it is to succeed.
There simply is no substitute
for doing all that is possible
to please the customer.

Jack A. Robinson
Chairman & C.E.O.
Perry Drug Stores, Inc.
Retail drug store chain

Customer satisfaction is
the by-product of putting the
needs and desires of customers
ahead of all other considerations.
Pier 1 Imports focuses its market strategy
to *exceed* expectations of every customer
in product selection and availability,
merchandise value and customer service.
The winning formula for retailers in the 1990's
is paying careful attention to customers.

Clark A. Johnson
Chairman & C.E.O.
Pier 1 Imports, Inc.
Retail home furnishings

In order to truly satisfy customers,
it is necessary
to understand their thoughts,
identify their needs
and then respond with solutions
that deliver innovative quality products,
systems and services.

George B. Harvey
Chairman, President & C.E.O.
Pitney Bowes, Inc.
Multinational manufacturing and marketing company

The customer is
the most important person
in any retail environment.
Sometimes we forget
that important point.
We must always do what is necessary
to keep the customer
coming back for more.

William V. Roberti
President & C.O.O.
Plaid Clothing Group
Men's tailored clothing manufacturer

Customer satisfaction is simple.
Think of how you want to be treated
and treat everyone that way
as often as possible.
Do this when things go badly
as much as it may hurt or embarrass you.
The great thing about this is
it pays off fiscally and emotionally.

Ara Kazanjian
President
Planet Micro
PC resellers and consultants

Meeting customers' expectations
is an important first step
in achieving customer satisfaction.
Continually exceeding
their expectations is the ultimate
customer satisfaction goal.

I. MacAllister Booth
Chairman, President & C.E.O.
Polaroid Corporation
Worldwide leader in instant imaging

Only the customer,
meaning each and every customer,
can define customer satisfaction.
Because customers'
needs and expectations vary,
a 100% Guarantee of Satisfaction
will allow each customer
to define satisfaction for you.

Michael D. Rose
Chairman
Promus Companies, Inc.
Casino entertainment and hotel development

We'd better
take care of our customers,
or someone else will.

Gary Richard
President & C.E.O.
P.C. Richard & Son, Inc.
*Retail electronics, appliances, and
home office products*

120

Better, Better, Best.
Don't settle for less, till better is Best.

Gary Richard
President & C.E.O.
P.C. Richard & Son, Inc.
*Retail electronics, appliances, and
home office products*

121

Customer satisfaction is
measuring our performance
not just on what the customer has
historically expected and received
but based on a broader definition of
need fulfillment.

Customer satisfaction is
working with the customer team
to identify unmet needs,
develop ways to meet these
and then measuring our success.

Phillip D. Ashkettle
President & C.E.O.
Reichhold Chemicals, Inc.
Polymers and polymer systems

... reaction ... relationship ...
price ... performance ... ambiance ...
Customer satisfaction is a perception
on the part of the end user
of the service or product
that for the price paid,
value is received,
and all other aspects of performance,
such as warranty service,
are achieved to a
high level of satisfaction.

Victor K. Kiam II
Chairman & C.E.O.
Remington Products, Inc.
Electric shavers, personal care and related products

We direct our efforts to the service of others,
first and foremost our customers.

We highly value the well-being
and success of our internal customers,
which will help us exceed the expectations
of our external customers.

We are committed to
exceed our customers' expectations
by understanding their current needs
and anticipating their future desires.

We listen and respond to our customers
and believe in open and honest communications.

from the booklet titled:
Our Vision, Mission & Values
Reynolds Metals Company
Aluminum and plastic products

124

Quite simply,
it's our mission, stated as follows:
"Roadway Services, Inc.,
through its operating companies,
IS IN THE BUSINESS
OF SATISFYING CUSTOMERS
by meeting their requirements
for value added transportation and
logistics services, thereby creating
value for our shareholders."

Joseph M. Clapp
Chairman & C.E.O.
Roadway Services, Inc.
Transportation and logistics businesses

Operate your company like a
"nudist colony"
where you hide nothing
from your clients.
They will quickly feel comfortable
being just as open with you.
This straightforward environment
has to begin with the sales process
and continue through to the
end of each transaction,
including your suppliers' part
in what you do.

Hal F. Rosenbluth
President & C.E.O.
Rosenbluth International
Travel management

I would define "customer satisfaction"
as being the natural result of
a consumer buying a product or service
which embodies a higher level of value
than the consumer anticipated.
Value is widely acknowledged to consist of the best
combination of price, quality, timeliness, and service.
When these attributes of value are truly in
optimal balance (price, for example, in accord with
quality), and a dash of innovation is added,
a product or service is transformed into an
extraordinary value which delights consumers.
And it is their delight which creates customer
satisfaction and repeat business.

Wolfgang R. Schmitt
Chairman & Chief Executive Officer
Rubbermaid Incorporated
Manufacturer of plastic and rubber products

Our customers' satisfaction
must drive the planning and
execution of our business.
We believe that by focusing
on customer value we will, in fact,
drive shareholder value.

M. Anthony Burns
Chairman, President & C.E.O.
Ryder Systems, Inc.
Transportation and logistics services

Customer satisfaction begins
with a reliable, quality product designed
to meet the needs of its end user.
A product should have a suitable feature package
and simple functions.
From there, the critical elements of satisfaction lie
in an easy-to-read owner's manual,
a convenient 800#, helpful customer service
representatives and fully-trained service centers.
The customer must feel proud of their purchase
and gratified with the service they received,
if assistance is necessary.

Albert Kim
President
Samsung Electronics America, Inc.
Consumer electronics and computer products

Customer satisfaction is nothing new.
We believe that customers,
regardless of what product or service they buy,
expect to be satisfied.
The challenge is to exceed those expectations —
to not merely achieve "customer satisfaction"
but "customer enthusiasm."

Richard G. LeFauve
President
Saturn Corporation
Automotive

A customer is satisfied
whenever his or her needs,
real or perceived, are met or exceeded.
Ask your customers what they want,
need and expect,
and then provide that and more.
Ask your customers continuously;
expectations change constantly.
Never feel like you have
done all that you can;
challenge yourself to do more.

Chuck Ferries
Chairman
Scott Sports Group
Schwinn Cycling & Fitness and Scott USA products

Customer satisfaction is not the goal;
providing a product or service
that is better than what the customer expected,
making your product a memorable, happy surprise
should be the goal.
In other words do more
than just "satisfy" the customer.

Tom Kalinske
President & C.E.O.
SEGA of America, Inc.
Video games and interactive software

"Treat every customer
like a guest in your home,"
has been the standard
my Dad established early on,
and it's still the backbone
of Service Merchandise!

Raymond Zimmerman
Chairman, President & C.E.O.
Service Merchandise
Catalog store retailer

At ServiceMaster
our goal is to ensure
that our customer's perception
of value in relation to cost
is always positive —
their satisfaction is our success.
The key is well-prepared and
empowered employees
willing to take responsibility
for perfection.

Carlos Cantu
President & Chief Executive Officer
ServiceMaster
Diversified services

134

A difficult message to communicate
to your company people is:
"Keeping your customers' goodwill
for the long term is probably
more important than any short-term gain."
Control your impulse to protect the company,
and ask yourself,
"Am I creating a customer for the long term,
or losing one?"

Richard J. Thalheimer
Chairman & C.E.O.
The Sharper Image Corporation
Specialty retailer and catalog mail order of unique products

Every taxpayer
deserves to be treated
like a customer.

Philip Lader
Administrator
Small Business Administration
*Financial and management assistance for
small businesses*

136

A little story
about customer satisfaction.
When we launched Snapple in Canada,
an outraged consumer called from Quebec,
complaining that the French on our label was lousy.
We called him immediately,
apologized for the error, and assured him
that all future labels would bear his correction.
He became a customer for life
that very moment.

Hyman Golden
Chairman
Snapple Beverage Corporation
Snapple natural beverages

Southwest Airlines
has two Customer types —
external and internal.
Passengers pay our way —
they are *external* Customers.
Employees are *internal* Customers.
As C.E.O., I must
endeavor to satisfy both.
Dissatisfied internal Customers
generally care little if they
provide satisfactory service.
Ergo, all Customers eventually
become unhappy.

Herb D. Kelleher
Chairman & President
Southwest Airlines
Commercial airline service

Business is a human experience
and we look at our company
as a social entity comprised of
various people groups:
employees, customers, dealers,
suppliers and stockholders.
In satisfying our customers, we have to
also balance the needs of all other
people groups so that collectively
we can continuously
improve quality
to the ultimate customer.

Robert C. Pew
Chairman
Steelcase, Inc.
Office furniture

Follow the "Golden Rule."
Design, produce, deliver and service
a product the way we would like it
and provide our customers
with the immediate means to satisfaction
by molding our toll free 800#
into every product we produce.
By focusing on the end consumer
we better serve the long term needs
of our retail customers.

Thomas G. Murdough, Jr.
President
Step 2 Corporation
Quality plastic products for children, home, and garden

We believe customer satisfaction is
earned the old fashioned way —
one day at a time.
You've got to constantly
listen to your customers,
and demonstrate a passion
to innovate and change your business
to meet their evolving needs.
In other words, you've got to
be willing to break things
long before they're broken —
because if you don't,
someone else will certainly do it for you.

John E. Martin
President & C.E.O.
Taco Bell Corporation
Quick service Mexican restaurants

141

Do what is right for the customer.

Corporate credo
Talbots, Inc.
Specialty apparel retailer

142

Whether it competes
in a global marketplace, as Texaco does,
or in a single locality,
a company must satisfy its customers,
individual by individual, if it is to succeed.
In our intensely competitive industry,
we must respond
to the needs of each customer
the first time and every time,
because we may not get
a second chance.

Alfred C. DeCrane, Jr.
Chairman & C.E.O.
Texaco, Inc.
Fuels and lubricants

Many organizations
have satisfied customers.
To me, satisfied customers are boring.
Rather, we should all want
Customer Enthusiasm.
When we truly serve and exceed
our customers' needs,
they are not satisfied,
they are enthusiastic
about their experience with us.
Only then have we done our job.

Douglas B. Leeds
President
Thomson-Leeds Co., Inc.
Point of purchase advertising

Satisfied customers
are those who not only accomplish,
but exceed their business plans
and recognize you as having played
an indispensable roll in those achievements.
Customers expect on-time deliveries
and high quality, but true partners
have a far deeper comprehension
of a customer's needs
and bring unremitting value
to his bottom line.

Joseph F. Toot, Jr.
President & C.E.O.
The Timken Company
Tapered roller bearings and alloy steels

Customer service is best described
as an opportunity —
a chance to evoke positive change
through cooperation and teamwork.

Gerald Greenwald
Chairman & C.E.O.
United Air Lines, Inc.
World's largest air passenger and cargo carrier

The Federal Government
must be
customer-driven.

President Bill Clinton
United States of America

Satisfying our customers
means we must listen to what they say;
find out what they want;
develop products or services
which meet their needs and wants;
provide the best possible product
and service delivery at reasonable prices,
and *always* follow-up
to see how we are doing.

Robert T. Herres
Chairman & C.E.O.
U.S.A.A.
Insurance and financial services

Customer satisfaction
is achieved through
determining and understanding
customer's needs and expectations
and providing goods and services
which meet them.

John G. Medlin, Jr.
Chairman
Wachovia Corporation
Financial services

Stop thinking
"customer satisfaction,"
start thinking
"customer enrichment."
A blind focus on customer satisfaction
binds a business to the here and now,
to articulated customer needs.
"Customer enrichment" leaps over
the paradigms of the present
to new technologies, new products,
new approaches and, ultimately,
wonderful new markets.

Melvin R. Goodes
Chairman & C.E.O.
Warner-Lambert Company
*Devoted to discovering, developing, manufacturing, and
marketing quality pharmaceutical, consumer health care,
and confectionery products*

In a commodity market
"Quality" is the differentiator.
It's the ticket to admission,
but more importantly,
the ride to long term success!

Charles A. Haggerty
Chairman & President
Western Digital Corporation
Disk drives and microcomputer products

151

Customer satisfaction means
something different to every guest
who walks into any of our 73 hotels
and resorts worldwide.
It's whatever a particular guest
says it is on any given day.
That's why it's so important
that associates are truly empowered
to meet our guests' expectations on the terms
the guests use to define customer satisfaction.
A guest satisfied with the accommodations and
services we provide day in and day out
is the one who will come back and contribute
to our continued success.

Jim Treadway
President
Westin Hotel Company
Westin hotels and resorts

Current, past and potential customers
define our business.
They are the reason we exist.
To be successful,
all our business efforts must be viewed
through the eyes of our customers.

Paul A. Allaire
Chairman & C.E.O.
Xerox Corporation
Document processing office equipment and services

About the Author

Armen J. Kabodian is an award-winning Senior Client Manager at IBM, where he services the Ford Motor Company account. He has received IBM's prestigious Golden Circle award three times. For this book, he asked 1000 leaders of major organizations to share their thoughts on customer satisfaction, customer service, and customer relations. From their responses, he selected more than 150 quotes that make up this book. He resides in Southeastern, Michigan, with his wife and two children.

Correspondence:

> Armen J. Kabodian
> P.O. Box 58
> Novi, MI 48376-0058
> or
> kabodian@interramp.com